STORIES OF
SHARING

SOCIAL EMOTIONAL LIBRARY

Published in the United States of America by Cherry Lake Publishing
Ann Arbor, Michigan
www.cherrylakepublishing.com

Content Adviser: Satta Sarmah Hightower, www.sattasarmah.com
Reading Adviser: Marla Conn MS, Ed., Literacy specialist, Read-Ability, Inc.

Photo Credits: ©Odua Images/Shutterstock Images, cover, 1; ©Donald Yip/Shutterstock Images, 5; ©USCapitol/Flickr, 7; ©f11photo/Shutterstock Images, 8; ©Amee Cross/Shutterstock Images, 11; ©ZUMA Press, Inc. / Alamy Stock Photo, 12; ©LembiBuchanan/iStock Images, 16; ©Obama White House/Flickr, 15; ©Frederic Legrand – COMEO/Shutterstock Images, 17; ©Michael Hsing/Wikimedia, 18; ©Anjo Kan/Shutterstock Images, 21; ©think4photop/Shutterstock Images, 22; ©Africa Studio/Shutterstock Images, 25; ©ARENA Creative/Shutterstock Images, 27; ©nito/Shutterstock Images, 28

Library of Congress Cataloging-in-Publication Data
Names: Colby, Jennifer, 1971- author.
Title: Stories of sharing / by Jennifer Colby.
Description: Ann Arbor : Cherry Lake Publishing, [2018] | Series: Social emotional library |
    Audience: Grade 4 to 6. | Includes bibliographical references and index.
Identifiers: LCCN 2017035925 | ISBN 9781534107472 (hardcover) | ISBN 9781534109452 (pdf) |
    ISBN 9781534108462 (pbk.) | ISBN 9781534120440 (hosted ebook)
Subjects: LCSH: Sharing—Juvenile literature.
Classification: LCC BF575.S48 C65 2018 | DDC 177/.7—dc23
LC record available at https://lccn.loc.gov/2017035925

Cherry Lake Publishing would like to acknowledge the work of The Partnership for 21st Century Learning.
Please visit *www.p21.org* for more information.

Printed in the United States of America
Corporate Graphics

ABOUT THE AUTHOR

Jennifer Colby is a school librarian in Michigan. She shares her time by volunteering
for organizations in her community.

TABLE OF CONTENTS

What Is Sharing?

Do you let classmates use your colored pencils for a school project? Do you give half your sandwich to a friend who forgot to bring lunch? Do you let your brother play games on your tablet? If so, then you are sharing. You can share many things, such as money, time, knowledge, and food. You can easily share with a friend or a neighbor, but you can also share with people on the other side of the world. Many people share what they have with people who have less. Sharing, whether it's a lot or a little, helps others.

Sharing means making sure everyone has what they need.

Benjamin Franklin

Benjamin Franklin, born January 17, 1706, became one of the Founding Fathers of the United States. Known as an inventor, **statesman**, and publisher, Franklin devoted his later years to **philanthropy**. His efforts to share his time, knowledge, and wealth helped make America what it is today.

In his late forties, Franklin had great success in the publishing business and in real estate, and he was one of the wealthiest men in the American colonies. He retired from business and devoted himself to public service. During the Revolutionary War, he became the ambassador to France and gained support for American independence from the French government. After the war, he helped to arrange peace with the British.

Franklin donated to any religious group that needed his help.

Throughout his life, he played a key role in creating many institutions in Philadelphia. He helped establish a lending library, a volunteer fire department, and a university that was open to all young men and not just the sons from privileged families. He also created the first charitable hospital, which treated all patients whether they could pay for services or not.

He donated large amounts of money and time to many worthy causes, including churches, synagogues, universities, and efforts to end slavery. He once said, "It is **prodigious** the quantity of

Franklin created a group called the Junto who wanted to improve Philadelphia.

good that may be done by one man, if he will make a business of it." Franklin created the concept of the matching grant. It's when one person's donation is matched by another donor up to a certain amount. It encourages people to donate to charitable causes.

Even after Franklin's death, his money was still going to good causes. In life, he had put money into two **trusts**: one for his birth city of Boston and one for his adopted city of Philadelphia. Most of the funds were not allowed to be spent for 200 years. In 1908, the city of Boston used its funds to start a trade school called the Benjamin Franklin Institute of Technology. In 1990,

Franklin's trusts matured, reaching their total value of $6.5 million. The city of Philadelphia used its funds to give scholarships to those looking to learn a trade, or to develop skills to do certain jobs.

Beyond all of his philanthropic efforts, Benjamin Franklin is best known for his diplomatic and advisory roles in the fight for American independence. He once said that the new democratic form of government could only survive if people were **virtuous**. Franklin's contributions to American society were enormous. Many believe that without his influence, guidance, and support, the American way of life would not be what it is today.

Do You Share with Others?

Has a friend ever asked to borrow something from you? If you let them use it, then you have shared it with them. Sometimes when we share something, we don't expect to get it back. But sometimes we do. Do you want what you shared back, or don't you? It is important to be clear about this at the start. Make sure that people understand what the expectations of sharing are. Clear communication keeps everyone happy.

Oseola McCarty

Not everyone has a lot of money to give away. Yet those people still choose to share what they have with others. Oseola McCarty, a washerwoman from Hattiesburg, Mississippi, donated $150,000 of her life savings to the University of Southern Mississippi to start a scholarship fund.

Born in 1908, McCarty left school in the sixth grade to take care of an elderly relative and never went back. She became a washerwoman like her grandmother and washed the clothes of teachers, doctors, lawyers, and police officers. She never married and never had any children, but she kept busy with her work.

McCarty was extremely **frugal** her entire life. She saved every penny she could in her bank account. She never subscribed to the

McCarty spent her time washing clothes by hand, not with a machine.

newspaper and never owned a car. She lived alone in her family's home and went on vacation only once in her lifetime. When her banker asked what she wanted to do with the growing sum of money in her account, she decided to give it to a local university. She claimed it was more money than she could ever use.

McCarty decided that the money would be for scholarships to the University of Southern Mississippi, and a fund was set up in her name. The scholarships would go to African-American students who could not otherwise afford to go to college.

McCarty started saving money when she was around eight years old.

In the 1960s, she saw the formerly **segregated** university accept black students for the first time. An official at the school said of McCarty, "She's seen the poverty, the young people who have struggled, who need an education. She is the most unselfish individual I have ever met."

The local community was surprised and delighted to hear of what they called "The Gift." Business leaders in Hattiesburg matched her donation to raise the fund to $300,000. News of her **generosity** spread around the nation, and she received many awards honoring her unselfish spirit. In 1995, President Bill Clinton awarded McCarty the Presidential Citizens Medal for admirable deeds to her fellow citizens. During an interview, she said, "I know it won't be too many years before I pass on … and I just figured the money would do them a lot more good than it would me."

By giving away her life's savings, Oseola McCarty was not only sharing her good fortune with others, but also benefiting from the gift herself. When asked by a reporter why she wasn't spending her savings on herself, she replied, "I am spending it on myself."

In 1995, at the age of 87, she met the first student to receive help from the Oseola McCarty Scholarship Fund, Stephanie Bullock—who treated her generous **benefactor** like a grandmother. McCarty died shortly after that, in 1999.

Warren Buffett and Bill Gates

There are people in this world who have billions of dollars. And there are two Americans who have given away billions of dollars to charity. Warren Buffett and Bill Gates have had very successful careers and not only share their money with charities around the world, but have pledged to share much more.

Born in 1930, Warren Buffett is a longtime investor and has made the majority of his fortune by buying and selling **stocks**. He has promised to give away 99 percent of his fortune to charitable causes during his lifetime or when he dies. A frugal person with a **net worth** of almost $73.7 billion, he lives in the same house that he purchased in 1958. He believes in getting his money's worth and does not spend it on useless things.

Buffett met with President Barack Obama in the Oval Office in 2010.

He eats at McDonald's and occupies most of his workday reading. He has also played a card game called bridge with Bill Gates.

Born in 1955, Bill Gates co-founded Microsoft, now the world's largest software company. With a net worth of almost $90 billion, Gates and his wife, Melinda, started the Bill and Melinda Gates Foundation in 2000. The goals of the foundation are to improve health care, reduce poverty worldwide, to expand educational opportunities, and to improve access to information technology in the United States.

The foundation donates money to help students who need to pay for college.

In 1991, Buffett became a **mentor** for Gates. When Gates established his foundation, he looked to Buffett for advice and included him on the board of trustees. Both men have made a commitment to giving away their fortunes and are encouraging others to do the same. Buffett and Gates created a promise called The Giving Pledge, and Facebook co-creator Mark Zuckerberg joined them in 2010. The Giving Pledge is a promise made by some of the world's wealthiest people to give away at least half of their money to charity.

The foundation also tries to improve health care around the world.

Over 100 billionaires have joined Gates and Buffett and promised
to donate at least half of their wealth.

In an interview, Gates once said about Buffett, "He goes out of his way to make people feel good about themselves and share his joy about life." Ranked as the top two philanthropists worldwide, both men bring immense joy to others. Buffett has donated more than $30 billion, and Gates has donated more than $29 billion to charitable causes. Through their efforts to share their vast fortunes with those less fortunate, both Warren Buffett and Bill Gates represent the true spirit of sharing.

Sharing in the Workplace

Sharing is an important part of having a successful career—no matter when you work. Practice now! Lending someone supplies or sharing ideas may not seem like a big deal, but behavior like this helps you become more generous and cooperative. People appreciate and respect those who share. In fact, sharing can encourage others to share with you when you need something. Additionally, sharing belongings or even stories can help you make new friends you wouldn't otherwise know. Maybe someone you don't know yet likes the same book as you or has a similar story to share!

Barton Brooks

It's easy to give away money when you have lots of it, but what if you have none? Starting with almost nothing, Barton Brooks now travels the world helping others in need. He calls his brand of philanthropy "**guerrilla** aid." He helps where it is needed, one small project at a time. He has generously shared his time and efforts, which has been an inspiration for others to do the same.

Brooks has been referred to as "a one-man international aid organization." Uninterested in traditional career paths, he tried many things over the years while looking for his passion. On a trip to Cambodia, he found it: helping others who have nothing. He returned home and wanted to "do something." He called a few aid groups but found that the type of individual help he wanted to give was not possible through large organizations.

Many refugees must travel across water to reach safety.

He decided to do the work on his own. With nothing to his name but a sports car that he built himself, he sold it and used the money to pursue his goal: bringing about change through unique and specific volunteer projects that help those who need it most anywhere in the world.

Now he's a global traveler, raising money to donate things people need, such as books, wheelchairs, clothes, and even chickens. When he is not donating things, he is sharing his time by building schools, digging toilet facilities, or doing whatever else is needed. He describes his approach as "the unconventional

Guerrilla Aid helped out after an earthquake happened in Nepal in 2015.

means with which a small group of volunteers use **mobile** tactics to combat a larger, less mobile, formal issue or problem." He believes that uncommon methods and smaller organizations can more effectively help others.

Others joined Brooks's effort and began the Guerrilla Aid organization. The group is able to take on larger projects. Its volunteers have worked with Syrian refugee children in Lebanon, not only providing schooling programs but also figuring out their physical and **psychological** needs. After a terrible earthquake in Nepal in 2015, Guerrilla Aid went to work helping to rebuild the city and aid its children.

Brooks's low-key generous lifestyle has brought him unexpected recognition. He was an advisor on human rights to the United Nations. He was a guest at the White House in 2007 for the United States's first World Malaria Day and personally greeted First Lady Laura Bush in Senegal for the start of one of her **goodwill** African tours. "That's how I see world change," Brooks said in an interview. "All of us taking responsibility for just doing something, large or small, to help someone with different challenges than our own." Despite not having much money to give, Barton Brooks chooses to share all he has with everyone he can.

CHAPTER 6

Food Charity

Have you ever been hungry? Hopefully when you are, you can just open your refrigerator and grab something to eat. But there are many people who do not know where their next meal will come from. To help their neighbors, restaurant owners and community organizations have come up with unique ways to share leftover food with those who need it.

An anonymous man in Saudi Arabia set up a charity refrigerator outside of his house. He put spare food in the fridge and encouraged his neighbors to do the same. To his surprise, dishes of freshly cooked food started showing up in the refrigerator. Now, people who live in his neighborhood who struggle to find food to eat have access to a fully stocked fridge.

One out of every nine people doesn't have enough to eat.

The idea of a charity refrigerator has become so popular that people all over the world are installing them.

Pappadavada, a restaurant in India, set up a refrigerator on the street outside its front door and encourages customers to put their leftovers in it. The restaurant also puts unsold food in the refrigerator. People in need just come and take it. The fridge is available 24 hours a day, seven days a week, and is never locked. Minu Pauline, who runs the restaurant, asks diners to write the date on their leftover food so that those who take it know how old it is. But she says food never stays in there very long, and the fridge regularly needs to be restocked. Pauline adds up to 100 servings of leftover food per day to share with those who need it.

Sometimes a business has more leftover food than it can handle. There are many organizations in the world that will pick up leftover food from local restaurants, grocery stores, farms, and hospitals. They deliver that food to churches, shelters, and community centers where it is served, so the food doesn't go to waste. The mission of one such organization—Food Gatherers in Ann Arbor, Michigan—is to "**alleviate** hunger and eliminate

Sharing extra food with others keeps it from going to waste.

Food Gatherers saves food from stores and restaurants from being thrown away.

its causes in our community." Food Gatherers picks up and distributes 6.4 million pounds of food annually to 150 partner organizations that serve the food to those in need.

There are many hungry people in the world, but there are many individuals and groups active in alleviating hunger. It can be as simple as giving leftover food to a hungry person, or it can involve hundreds of volunteers who pick up and deliver food that would otherwise go to waste. The main goal of these efforts is to provide needed food to others by sharing what is already available.

What Have You Learned About Sharing?

There are many ways to share. People who have a lot of money to give away can help solve major problems like poverty and disease. People who share their time can help someone less fortunate to get something done. Many people benefit from the generosity of others—it is what makes this world a better place. What can you do to share what you have with others? Ask your parents how you can help people in your community by sharing your time, old clothes or toys, or even some of your birthday money. Sharing what you have brings joy to others. And stop and think about this: How does sharing make you feel?

Think About It

How Can You Share More with Others?

Think about extra things that you might have. Do you have some clothes that you have grown out of? Do you have toys that you don't want anymore? Maybe you can give those items to others who need them. That is an easy way to share. Or you could share your time by helping an elderly neighbor do yardwork or clean. Ask your parents how you can share what you have with others.

For More Information

Further Reading

Lewis, Barbara A. *The Kid's Guide to Service Projects: Over 500 Service Ideas for Young People Who Want to Make a Difference.* Minneapolis: Free Spirit Publishing, 2009.

McCarty, Oseola. *Simple Wisdom for Rich Living.* Atlanta: Longstreet Press, 1996.

Smith, Daniel. *How to Think Like Bill Gates.* London: Michael O'Mara Books Ltd., 2015.

Websites

The Giving Pledge—A Commitment to Philanthropy
https://givingpledge.org/
Check out the official website of The Giving Pledge, which highlights pledgers and their reasons for doing so.

Guerrilla Aid—Direct & Effective Funding
www.guerrillaaid.org
Learn more about the philanthropic organization established by Barton Brooks.

Philanthropy Roundtable—Philanthropy Hall of Fame
www.philanthropyroundtable.org/almanac/hall_of_fame
Use this website to learn more about great acts of philanthropy by people who have passed away.

GLOSSARY

alleviate (uh-LEE-vee-eyt) to make something less severe

benefactor (BEN-uh-fak-tur) someone who helps another person or group by giving money

frugal (FROO-guhl) not wasteful; using money wisely

generosity (jen-uh-RAH-sih-tee) the quality of being kind, understanding, and not selfish

goodwill (gud-WIL) a kindly feeling of support and cooperation

guerrilla (guh-RIL-uh) refers to the actions of a small group of people who do things as an independent unit

mentor (MEN-tor) someone who gives advice to a less experienced and often younger person

mobile (MOH-buhl) able to move or be moved easily

net worth (NET WURTH) the remainder of what is owned by someone after subtracting what they owe

philanthropy (fuh-LAN-thruh-pee) the practice of giving money or time to help make life better for other people

prodigious (pruh-DIJ-uhs) enormous or amazing in amount

psychological (sye-kuh-LAH-jih-kuhl) of or relating to the mind

segregated (SEG-rih-gay-tid) kept separate or apart from the main group, often by race

statesman (STAYTS-muhn) a person respected for great experience and leadership in government

stocks (STAHKS) shares of the value of a company that can be bought, sold, or traded as an investment

trusts (TRUHSTS) special accounts with money that will go to someone else in the future, with certain rules attached

virtuous (VUR-choo-uhs) having high moral qualities

INDEX